Praise for *A Pebble for Your Thoughts*

"Small acts of kindness are one of the few things every person is capable of—regardless of age, geography, socioeconomic status, education, or occupation—it just takes intention. Teaching our children about their power to create positive ripples of hope every day and wherever they find themselves, and the cumulative impact of all those small acts of kindness is one of the most powerful lessons we can impart to our children."

—Molly Yuska, Founder of Project Giving Kids

"Kindness is the great healer that lives inside of you. No matter what hardships you face—grief, anger, frustration, or despair—there is a part of you that is your own best friend, even if you have felt estranged from yourself for years. Welcome yourself back home, knowing that self-compassion is your birthright and your greatest resource. Offering yourself kindness is how you bear the unbearable, how you begin to heal yourself, and how you become a beacon of hope to other people in need. All you have to do is show you care."

—Heather Stang, MA, C-IAYT, author of *Mindfulness & Grief*

T0098803

"This idea is so right on so many levels. The tactile reminder of thoughts to enrich our lives. The unlimitedness of rocks similar to the abundant ways we can be more compassionate. And, I love its double message: physical rocks with meaningful messages, and, the fact that kindness truly does rock."

—Allen Klein, author of *The Art of Living Joyfully*

"Maybe the thing I love most of all is how these sweet rocks give people hope, sometimes when they need it the most: cancer patients, people who lost a loved one, someone suffering from depression and anxiety and those who feel lost and alone. This book will inspire you to make a difference in the world."

—Becca Anderson, author of *Real Life Mindfulness* and *Badass Affirmations*

"When you begin to focus on extending kindness toward others, you'll feel more kindness coming toward you. Every Kindness Rock creates a ripple of love and kindheartedness, spreading a positive message out into the world. Megan Murphy's marvelous book will not only teach you how to make these remarkable rocks but, more importantly, why you should create kindness rocks. What a wonderful way to share your heart!"

—Susyn Reeve, author of *Heart Healing* and *The Inspired Life*

"Megan Murphy actively makes the world a more loving, and less painful place. Her story and kindness rocks teach us that through helping others, we can find healing within ourselves."

—Kate Allan, author of *You Can Do All Things*

"As a prayer artist, I see each of these Kindness Rocks as a prayer. This book is a wonder and The Kindness Rocks Project is making the world a better place. Brava, Megan Murphy for this inspired idea!"

—Janet Conner, author of *Writing Down Your Soul*

"We are here to love 24/7 and kindness rocks spreads that in such a special way. The heart connections created by *A Pebble For Your Thoughts* and this important movement can help heal the world and bring more caring compassion between people, which is much needed now."

—Judy Ford, author of *Every Day Love*

A Pebble for Your Thoughts

How One Kindness Rock At the Right Moment Can Change Your Life

Megan Murphy

TURNER

PUBLISHING COMPANY

Turner Publishing
Nashville, Tennessee
www.turnerpublishing.com

Copyright © 2018 Megan Murphy.

Cover & Layout Design: Roberto Núñez
Cover Photo: Denise Barker Photography

No part of this publication may be reproduced, stored in a retrieval system, or transmitted in any form or by any means, electronic, mechanical, photocopying, recording, scanning, or otherwise, except as permitted under Sections 107 or 108 of the 1976 United States Copyright Act, without either the prior written permission of the Publisher, or authorization through payment of the appropriate per-copy fee to the Copyright Clearance Center, 222 Rosewood Drive, Danvers, MA 01923, (978) 750-8400, fax (978) 750-4744. Requests to the Publisher for permission should be addressed to Turner Publishing Company, 4507 Charlotte Avenue, Suite 100, Nashville, Tennessee, 37209, (615) 255-2665, fax (615) 255-5081, E-mail: admin@turnerpublishing.com.

Limit of Liability/Disclaimer of Warranty: While the publisher and the author have used their best efforts in preparing this book, they make no representations or warranties with respect to the accuracy or completeness of the contents of this book and specifically disclaim any implied warranties of merchantability or fitness for a particular purpose. No warranty may be created or extended by sales representatives or written sales materials. The advice and strategies contained herein may not be suitable for your situation. You should consult with a professional where appropriate. Neither the publisher nor the author shall be liable for any loss of profit or any other commercial damages, including but not limited to special, incidental, consequential, or other damages.

A Pebble for Your Thoughts: One Message at Just the Right Moment Can Change Someone's Entire Day, Outlook, Life!

*The messages on the rocks pictured in this book are written in shorthand so may contain grammatical, spelling, or punctuation inconsistencies.

Library of Congress Cataloging-in-Publication number: 2018960037
ISBN: (print) 978-1-63353-950-1, (ebook) 978-1-63353-951-8
BISAC category code: SEL004000 SELF-HELP / Affirmations

Printed in the United States of America

Table of Contents

Chapter 3
Grief and Healing

Foreword

Kindness is "love made visible" and that is exactly what these beautiful kindness rocks do. Even more so, they make kindness tangible. You can hold a kindness rock in your hand and keep it somewhere to be a daily reminder that there is a lot of good in the world. You can also leave it somewhere for somebody to find; somebody who might be hurting or grieving, struggling with illness, loss or great difficulty. Finding this message in the form of a kindness rock can uplift, offer cheer, healing, and make all the difference in someone's life. We have never needed kindness more than now. Megan Murphy and The Kindness Rocks Project are doing the very vital work of inspiring us and reminding of us of the "better angels of our nature." Now, take up take up your paint brushes and join the kindness rocks revolution!

RANDOM ACTS OF KINDNESS FOUNDATION

Introduction

As I stumble through this life,
help me create more laughter than tears,
dispense more happiness than gloom,
spread more cheer than despair.

Never let me become so indifferent,
that I will fail to see the wonders in the eyes of the child.
Or the twinkle in the eyes of the aged.

Never let me forget that my total effort is to cheer people,
make them feel happy, and forget momentarily,
all the unpleasantness in their lives.

And in my final moment,
may I hear you whisper:
"When you made my people smile,
you made me smile."

"The Clown's Prayer," Author Unknown

How it all began…

What started as the simple hobby of one, has now turned into an international grassroots kindness movement of many. Now, more than ever, people are longing for kindness and connection. During these uncertain times, we are inundated with daily news reports that focus on unsettling events and these images evoke a sense of fear and unease. I personally became affected by this when I began each day bombarded with negativity while watching the morning news, which I subconsciously carried with me throughout the day. As a result, I grew increasingly more pessimistic and apprehensive of others.

That is when I made the conscious decision to turn off the morning news and substitute it with daily morning walks on the beach. My outlook began to change almost immediately, and I discovered my yearning for inner peace. That is where my journey began and where The Kindness Rocks Project was born. I wanted to share my newfound positive outlook with others. I dared to dream that maybe, just maybe, I could make a difference and inspire others to do the same.

I began painting simple inspirational messages on rocks and dropping them along the beach on my morning walks. In the beginning, the messages were brief: *"you got this," "the answer lies within,"* or *"follow your heart."* I had no idea if anyone would ever find one of these messages. However, I had hopes that if they did, it would be viewed as a positive message that was meant just for them, or the sign they needed at just the right moment.

On the first day, I dropped only five rocks over a one-and-a-half mile stretch of rocky beach, and that evening I received a text message from a friend with a picture of one of those rocks. She asked if I had dropped the rock she had found on the beach that very same day. At first, I denied it because I felt strongly about maintaining anonymity. And what would people think about a forty-seven-year-old woman painting kindness rocks and leaving them along the beach? I feared that my actions would appear strange to people.

My friend had recognized my handwriting, so she knew it was me. It was what she said in her text that made me realize I had given her a gift, one that she greatly needed and appreciated. She said, "Well, if it was you that dropped it, I want to thank you because I was having a bad day and this little rock turned my day around."

This is the moment when I realized that others were also experiencing similar difficulties or life transitions and that a simple act of kindness could make a big difference. As a result of this epiphany, my personal hobby of painting messages on rocks turned into something so much bigger. I began painting and dropping more and more rocks in hopes that I could inspire others who needed a "message." I left them on the beach, at the grocery store, at the coffee shop, and basically anywhere I felt they would be found by someone who needed the inspiration.

The concept further manifested itself in the form of inspirational kindness rock gardens that I created around Cape Cod where people were encouraged to *"take one if you need one," "share one with a friend,"* or *"add one to the pile."* This idea spread quickly! Now other people were able to experience the same magic I had uncovered for myself.

Three years later, a hobby has turned into an international kindness movement. When I began posting these kindness rocks on social media, followers began sharing them. Schools, businesses and organizations picked up on the mission and joined to promote The Kindness Rocks Project initiative.

The Kindness Rocks Project provides a counteraction to all of the negativity swirling around our planet. The tagline for the project is *"one message at just the right moment can change someone's entire day, outlook, life."* Sometimes, all it takes is just one simple positive message to change your perspective.

Within the pages of this book, you may just find that perfect message at the exact moment in time when you are in need of it. I hope that you will reflect on that message and, once you have received the inspiration, take a moment to share that message with another human being...because you never know who is in need of a similar message and a touch of your kindness.

Chapter 1

Strength

Not all Storms come to disrupt your Life. Some come to clear your Path. ♥

"Not All Storms Come to Disrupt Your Life. Some Come to Clear Your Path."

—The Minds Journal

Some storms come into our lives as lessons. These life storms often blow in out of the clear blue sky, carrying winds of wisdom which ignite thunderbolts filled with great insight. There are many blessings we can extract from these life lessons. Often the timing could have been predicted if we paid attention to the warning signs. Along our journey, we were given small moments of insight that we simply ignored. We didn't pay attention to that gut feeling and as a result, another moment arose and we made the conscious decision to ignore it yet again, out of fear. That is why the "storm" hit. We must take some responsibility for not preparing for it. We may have actually convinced ourselves that we could outrun this storm. Trust that this storm blew in to help you, to move you further along your path. It simply cleared the way. You will now move forward with greater wisdom that you require to navigate further down the road of your life's journey.

Step Into Your Power: Now Is Your Time!

If you read the message on this rock and it hits you somewhere deep inside, enough to have an emotional reaction, then now is your time! Maybe you simply needed a boost of some sort to get you going. Consider this that long awaited moment of inspiration. Now is your time to step into that power of yours.

Sometimes the heroes need saving like the villains need love.

"Sometimes, the Heroes Need Saving Like the Villains Need Love."

Author Unknown

Often the heroes don't realize that they are the ones who need saving. The thing about heroes is that they are always helping others. They are selfless and compassionate and seek out those who may need their assistance. But the heroes often don't realize why they are this way, rather they just continue to act. A heroic act can be something small or unnoticed, but it is the impact of that act that makes it "heroic." It is in giving to others what we need ourselves that we heal and grow! Therefore, the heroes are not only saving others, but at the same time they are saving themselves.

Often our dark patches are actually the universe conspiring to point us in a new direction

Often Our Dark Patches Are Actually the Universe Conspiring to Point Us in a New Direction

Often we find ourselves in one of life's dark patches or we simply feel off. As if nothing is going right. These dark patches present themselves as a breeding ground for wisdom and personal growth. When we are able to look at these difficult times through curious eyes, we can begin to see the way out or the proverbial light at the end of the tunnel. These dark patches are the Universe's way of notifying us that we are off course, and maybe there's a better way. Get still. Listen deeply to your SELF and there you will find the wisdom or your personal GPS to help you navigate into the light and onto the path that was made just for YOU!

I Can Do Difficult Things!

Think of a time in your past when you didn't think you would get through whatever difficult times you were having. Remember how anxious you felt, full of fear of the unknown? Hey, you made it through for better or for worse, and you are here today. That is evidence in itself that you can do it again! You will OVERCOME many adverse moments in this amazing life of yours. Simply see them as minor obstacles or opportunities for personal growth so you can evolve and gain the tools you need to navigate the next one. Also, know that there are people in your life who care about you and would love to help in whatever way they can. Sometimes reaching out for that help IS the brave thing to do.

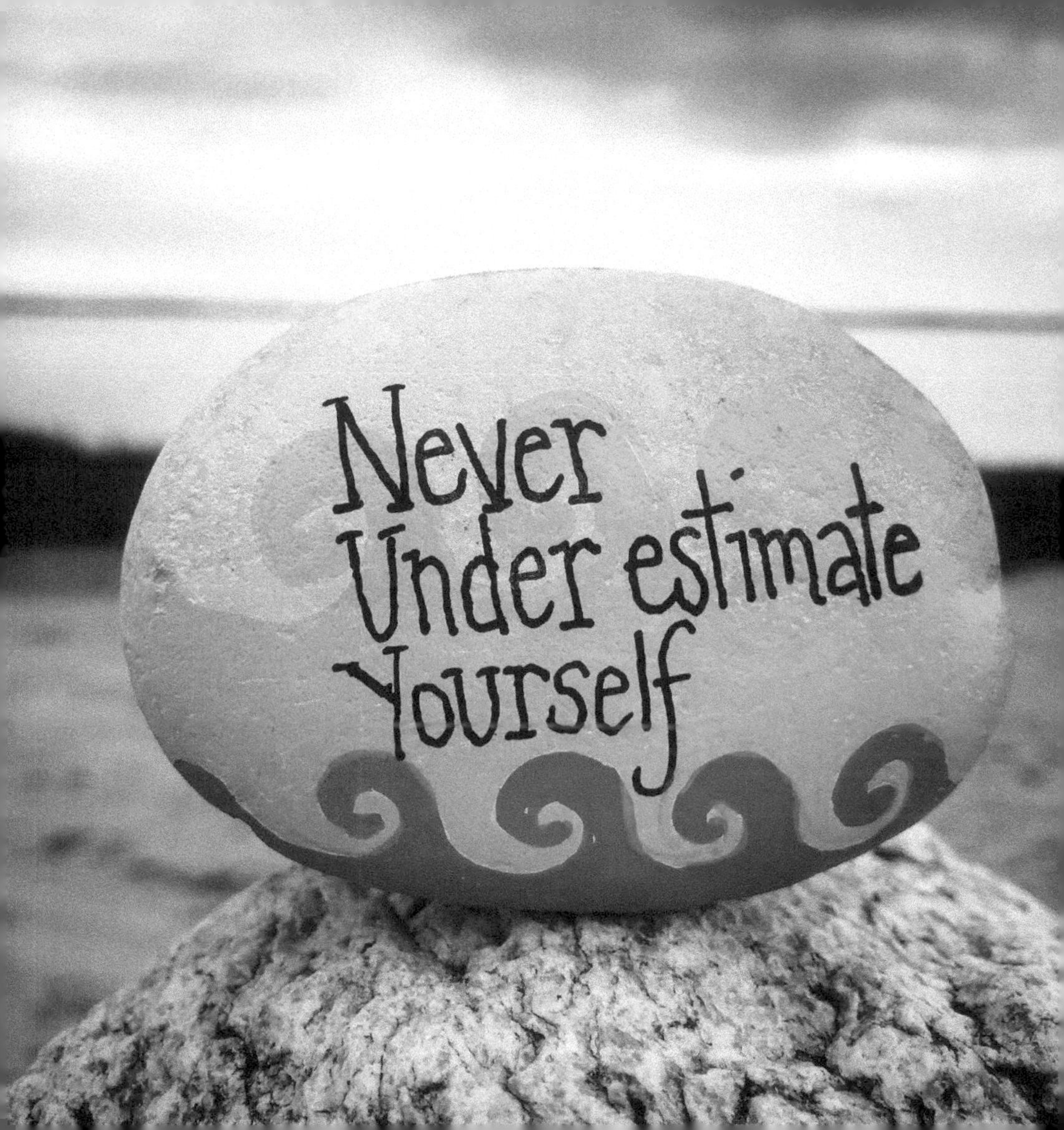
Never
Under estimate
Yourself

Never Underestimate Yourself!

Never underestimate yourself! I must say this can be tricky, right? One minute
we acknowledge our "value" and defend it at all costs, and the next, we knock
ourselves down internally with that self-critical talk of ours. Or we allow
ourselves to compare our value against another's. This is exhausting isn't it?
Here's the thing. YOU are VALUABLE in every way. In fact, there is no one
else in the entire world like you. Therefore, you can't get the role of you wrong,
right? So the good news is that all you need to do is to be you, show up, and
know that you are exactly where you should be in each moment because you
bring your unique self to any situation. This world needs all of us, the dreamers,
the doers, the worriers, the warriors, and everyone in between.

Calm Is My Superpower

There is great power in silence and remaining calm is a process. First, we must be aware that we are experiencing unease such as doubt, fear, anger, sadness, or frustration. That is a simple, yet important, part of the process. Once we understand what's happening, we can stop ourselves from getting hijacked by our negative emotions. Next, begin breathing mindfully, take slow deep breathes and pay attention to the breathing process. This will take us out of our head that is filling up with negative thoughts and keep us present. This is a pause, where we will then be able to respond rather than react to any difficult situation. We then begin moving out of "problem mode" and into "solution mode." Through our calm, we find that anything is possible.

Courage

Courage is that quiet voice deep within that whispers to us, "You have got this."
It is the catalyst for accomplishment! When we listen to that inner guidance and
go for it, we are flexing our resilience muscle. And whether we succeed or fail at
whatever it is we are attempting, in the end, we will feel proud of having tried.
Often, the simple act of leaning in and ignoring our fear is all of the strength
we need. This becomes a tool we can use moving forward for the next difficult
moment that arises down the road.

you never know how strong you are until being strong is the only choice you have.

"You Never Know How Strong You Are Until Being Strong Is the Only Choice You Have."

—Bob Marley

You are so much stronger than you think. Life often brings us moments and situations that test our strength. We wonder how or if we can make it through them. When we dig deep, go within and tap into our inner strength, we rise to meet each situation because we have no choice. And when we do, we are introduced to a part of ourselves we never knew. That strong, brave and powerful self that we have spent most of our lives trying to find. She reveals herself in these moments to show us that she has always been there. It is in these moments that we unlock that power and life becomes more beautiful. We stand a bit taller and walk a bit lighter. Wearing a smile that reveals that we have uncovered a beautiful secret. We can conquer the world!

Sometimes simply recognizing the Storm Allows it to pass.

Sometimes, Simply Recognizing the Storm Allows It to Pass

Simply being aware that we are in a "life storm" helps bring some perspective to the situation. Awareness is key. It is at this point in which we can detach from habitual negative thoughts that keep us stuck in it. Awareness helps us move to the next logical step which is decision making. We can then decide how we want to address it, moving out of reactive mode into responsive mode. Responsive mode enables us to focus our thoughts on a solution rather than on the negative, self-sabotaging thoughts which hold us back from growing, learning from our adversities and evolving.

Kites rise highest against the wind ~ not with it.
~Winston Churchill

"Kites Rise Highest Against the Wind, Not with It."
—Winston Churchill

It is in life's difficult moments that we gain our strength. Challenges present opportunities for growth and an expansion in perspective. It takes a pretty strong gust of wind to raise a kite so that the kite can soar. These are the winds of change we need to rise and then shine.

Be happy
for this moment.
This moment is
your Life.

~Omar Khayyam

"Be Happy for This Moment. This Moment Is Your Life."

—Omar Khayyam

In this very moment, we all have a choice. These choices are to embrace happiness, joy, courage and perseverance or to allow ourselves to become consumed with feelings such as anger, sadness and fear. We will never get this moment in time back again. Each moment is a gift and a blessing. Choose wisely!

Chapter Two

Encouragement

Keep Going

Keep going: You will get there!

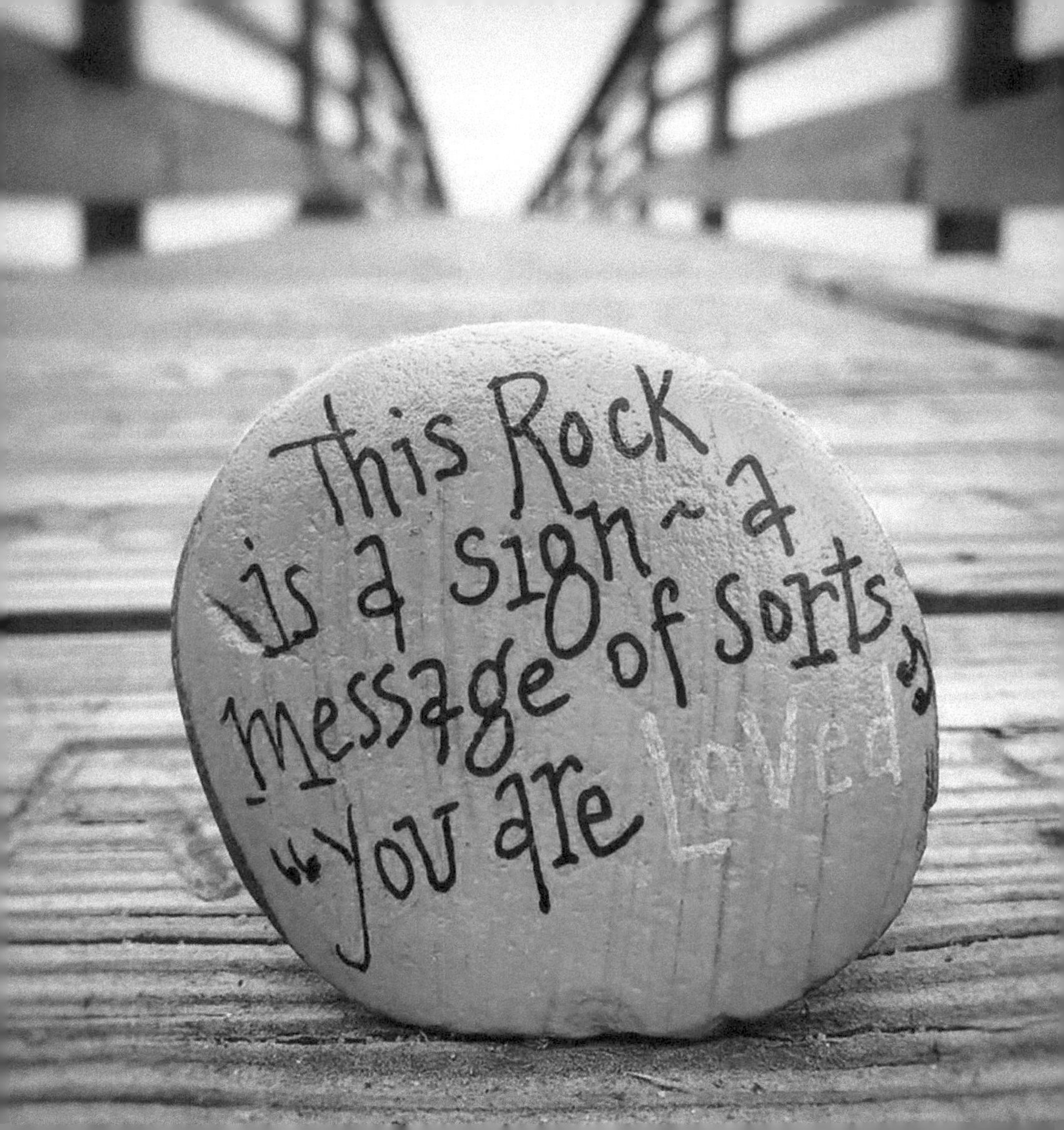
This Rock
is a sign ~ a
message of sorts;
"you are Loved"

This Rock Is a Sign, a Message of Sorts That You Are Loved

What if we all took the time to let one another know how much we care about them?

Often we think to ourselves, "wow, that person is great," "they are so confident and I love how they carry themselves," "how lovely is he/she," etc. But when we pause, we often lose the opportunity to express ourselves. It could be that we may feel funny or vulnerable about sharing our thoughts. Here's the thing—we must let others know that they matter. You may never know what is going on with someone else and your kind words could make all of the difference to them. Reflect upon a moment in time when someone shared a compliment with you. Remember how that compliment made you feel. Has there been a moment of self-doubt where you use the reminder of this compliment to provide you with confidence? Today, let someone know that you care. You will be surprised at how this simple act will make you feel better too.

Let the beauty of what you love be what you do

Rumi

"Let the Beauty of What You Love Be What You Do."

—Rumi

Each of us has our own individual purpose to fulfill in life. In uncovering what makes us happy, we then have a clearer understanding of what that purpose is. Pursue those things that you love to do, and you will love the life you live.

Be Positive!

Be in the habit of looking for the positive moments throughout your day and the positive moments will begin to present themselves to you.

Today will be a great day... I can and I will!

Today Will Be a Great Day...I Can and I Will!

Starting your day with a positive thought can make all of the difference. Give yourself a mini pep talk before heading out the door and begin to notice how your positive thoughts begin to manifest.

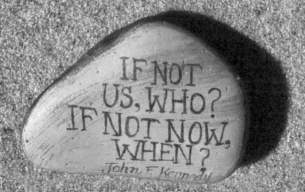

IF NOT
US, WHO?
IF NOT NOW,
WHEN?
John F. Kennedy

"If Not Us, Who? If Not Now, When?"

—John F. Kennedy

Today's call to action: each of us has an opportunity in each moment to choose. We get to choose by way of our virtues who we want to be and what we wish to stand for. The choice is ours and ours alone.

Hope

"We must accept finite disappointment, but never lose infinite hope."
—*Martin Luther King, Jr.*

when life gets blurry,
adjust your focus.

When Life Gets Blurry, Adjust Your Focus

Maybe this message comes to you today because you feel off course,
stuck or bored?

When life gets "blurry," we have lost our focus. It is important to realize that
OUR focus is individual and different than anyone else's. Rather than looking
around at what everyone else is doing, it is important for us to go within. Get
quiet, focus your attention on that tiny voice within. It is always there trying to
reach you. That inner wisdom has simply been buried underneath self-doubt
and fear and clouded by insecurity. Pay attention to your feelings. When you are
feeling anxious or sad or angry, it simply means you are off course and need to
redirect. Each of us has one purpose, which is happiness, however, our journey
in uncovering it is as individuals becomes our fingerprints.

Let your vision pull you.

Let Your Vision Pull You

What is your vision? Do you have one? Maybe you haven't uncovered yours yet. Maybe you had a different vision of what your life would look like. Perhaps you recognize that you possess a burning desire, but you are afraid to allow yourself to pursue it. Visions are powerful. They are created with intention. Go ahead and dream big and allow yourself to be pulled by that vision of yours.

believe
in yourself
&
you will be
unstoppable

Believe in Yourself and You Will Be Unstoppable

Be believable, be authentic, be you and you will be unstoppable!

now More then ever... Kindness can become a connecting force for good. ♥ TKPP

Now More than Ever, Kindness Can Become a Connecting Force for Good

When we show kindness toward others, we are creating greater connections and fostering goodwill which, in a nutshell, means that we become a connecting force for good!

"One Moment Can Change a Day, One Day Can Change a Life, and One Life Can Change the World."

—Buddha

One moment can change a day... Be on the lookout for these moments. Often we are not aware that there are signs and messages surrounding us throughout the day. When we experience problems, it is common that clues to solutions pop up. But we are often so consumed with the problem that we don't even notice.

One day can change a life... Just like that—in an instant, one day can change your life!

Life is precious, and we must remember to be grateful for what we have, and honor those whom we love. So too, in an instant, amazing opportunities could present themselves out of thin air almost magically. We must believe this is possible!

Finally, one life can change the world, and that life is yours. Just being YOU is making a difference in this world. Your mere existence has meaning and purpose in making this world a better place through your unique and kind spirit.

Chapter 3

Grief and Healing

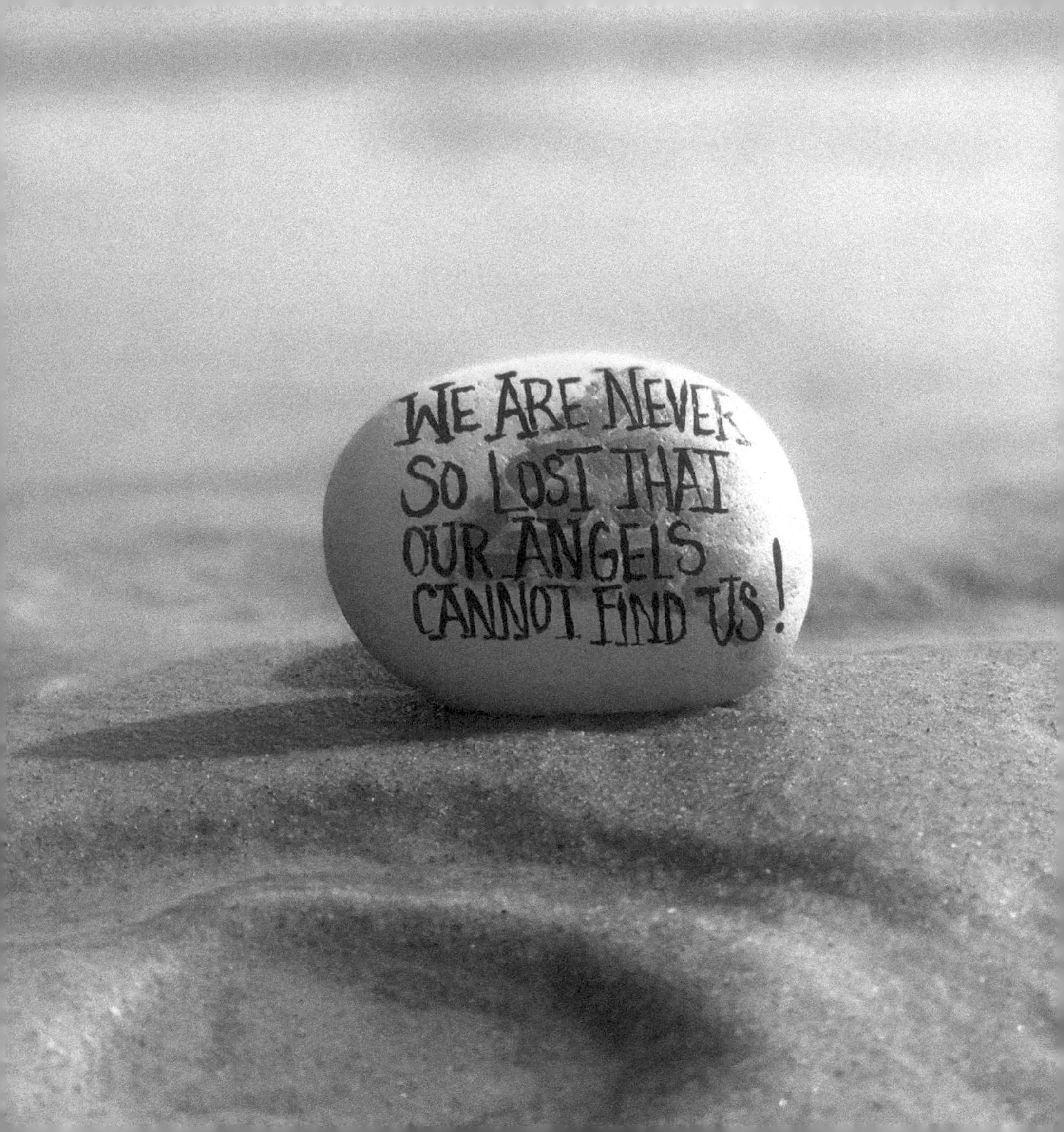
WE ARE NEVER
SO LOST THAT
OUR ANGELS
CANNOT FIND US!

We Are Never So Lost That Our Angels Cannot Find Us

Especially when we are feeling lost, it is our angels who walk beside us that make sure that we do not lose our way.

Your angels are with you, they just aren't leaving any footprints.

Your Angels Are with You, They Just Aren't Leaving Any Footprints.

If you have lost a loved one, there may be days when you feel connected to something or someone and you may be unable to figure out what "it" is. You never talk about it, or share it with anyone because you feel as if people may think that you are crazy. But there are things that happen such as coincidences, chance meetings, and synchronistic signs that appear. It may seem as if you are on candid camera and someone is trying to get a reaction out of you. However, after too many of these instances, you may begin to just let them happen and search for the deeper meaning behind such occurrences. You may even begin to embrace the signs as support and guidance from a loved one from above.

No one saves us but ourselves. No one can and no one may. We ourselves must walk the Path.

BUDDHA

"No One Saves Us but Ourselves. No One Can and No One May. We Ourselves Must Walk the Path."

—Buddha

We ourselves must walk the path. At times of crisis or in moments of fear, we often look to others to help solve our situation. This is a natural human response toward problem-solving. We expend so much energy into finding someone to "fix" our situation when we would be better off digging deep and problem solving ourselves. All of life's difficult moments are opportunities for personal growth. They help us evolve and gain the strength that we never realized we had all along. It is great to find support...someone to encourage or inspire us to act; however, WE must take the steps necessary to move forward and along the way we will pick up those life lessons necessary for future experiences. One day, we will look back and realize how each difficult experience prepared us for the next. It's all part of the journey called life.

These are the days that must happen to you.

~Walt Whitman

"These Are the Days That Must Happen to You."
—Walt Whitman

It is easier for us to embrace and accept the wonderful days. Those days when amazing things happen and we feel on top of our game, in flow and unstoppable! However, on those other days...you know which days I'm talking about...most of our days, filled with uninspired to-do lists, difficult life situations, and challenging relationships. We often don't realize their importance for our personal growth. These are the days that we must embrace and celebrate. These are the days where we are given the opportunity to "dig deep" and learn how to navigate ourselves back toward those seemingly better days. Or better yet, find our happiness within those uninspired moments. It is a process, a mindset based upon our state of awareness.

Love the people that God gave you, because he will need them back one day.

Love the People That God Gave You, Because He Will Need Them Back One Day

When I come to the end of the road
And the sun has set for me
I want no rites in a gloom filled room.
Why cry for a soul set free?

Miss me a little, but not too long
And not with your head bowed low.
Remember the love we once shared,
Miss me but let me go.

For this is a journey we all must take,
and each must go alone.
It's all a part of the master plan,
a step on the road to home.

When you are lonely or sick at heart
Go to the friends we know
And bury your sorrows in doing good deeds.
Miss me—but let me go.

Christina Rossetti, "Miss Me But Let Me Go"

When we Lose a Loved One, We Gain A Guardian Angel

When We Lose a Loved One, We Gain a Guardian Angel

"We cannot pass our guardian angel's bounds, resigned or sullen, he will hear our sighs."

—Saint Augustine

Kindness is ~~a~~ the cure!

Kindness Is the Cure!

What if kindness is THE cure? The cure to what ails us. Kindness has the power to heal. When we are feeling down, kindness has the power to lift our spirits through both giving and receiving. When we are in a state of crisis, a simple act of kindness from a stranger has the power to ignite an inner peace. Kindness can transform communities amidst great tragedy and loss and create greater bonds and connections. Finally, kindness is the unspoken language of love, which is Universal.

Sometimes, Something as Simple as a Smile Can Make All of the Difference

A smile can make all of the difference. It can make people feel a connection to one another, and this is especially impactful during those times when we may feel sad, overwhelmed or insecure. Imagine one of life's awkward moments... for example, the first day at a new school when you were a teenager. You were filled with self-consciousness and anxiety about not knowing anyone or where to go. A simple smile in this moment was a game changer, a lifeline of sorts. This simple gesture made you feel so much better. So today, go ahead and smile more. Some may not smile back, but you will leave them with a lovely feeling.

maybe, all of the confusing things happening in our world right now are simply preparing us for a kinder, more compassionate existance that's well overdue?

Maybe All of the Confusing Things Happening in Our World Right Now Are Preparing Us for a Kinder, More Compassionate Existence That's Well Overdue

Could it be that our world in which we live is ready for a recalibration?

Chapter 4

Faith

Sometimes what you're looking for comes when you're not looking!

Sometimes, What You're Looking for Comes When You're Not Looking!

Maybe you are looking too hard in one direction and what you are really looking for can be found in your peripheral vision. We get so focused on a particular goal or vision for our lives, keeping our sights set on achieving it. Although having a goal in mind is great, the "how" in terms of achieving it unfolds through persistence, faith and hard work. We must remember that we all have a higher purpose and most often it keeps trying to get our attention by way of synchronicities or coincidences and when we are too focused in one direction, we often miss these signs. It is quite possible that what you're looking for will simply come to you in the perfect timing for your highest good. If it came to you too early, it's possible that you were not ready for it to arrive. So stay mindful and be aware of your surroundings and interactions with people who come into your life. What you are looking for often finds you. The question is, will you even notice?

Something Great Is Headed Your Way, Be Patient and Remain Positive

Even when it seems as if nothing is going right…especially when it seems like everything is difficult and the chips are stacked against us, we must always trust and have faith and most importantly HOPE that things will eventually turn around. One tool that speeds up this process is simply adjusting our attitude and overall demeanor. When we spend time discussing with others our "problems," we then amplify them and make them bigger. We remain stuck in negative energy and draw others into that energy as well. We become a conduit drawing these situations to us. Adversely, if we remain positive and look for the lessons learned from difficult situations and search for the silver linings, we are able to pull ourselves out of that negative vibration into a more positive one and we then begin to attract or call in solutions and new positive insight.

Faith

Faith is believing in the possibility that whatever happens is happening to us for a reason. The things that come into our lives are either blessings or they carry great lessons. Faith is believing in this.

One day you will look back and realize the little things are the Big things

One Day, You Will Look Back and Realize the Little Things Are the Big Things

One day, we will look back and realize that the little things were really the big things all along. Today, embrace those little moments: the smile from an innocent child, the wag of a dog's tail, the wave from an elderly neighbor, your morning walk. These simple moments may seem routine now, but one day we will look back upon these moments through our mind's eye and they will make us smile. We may even wish we took the time to recognize how lovely they were.

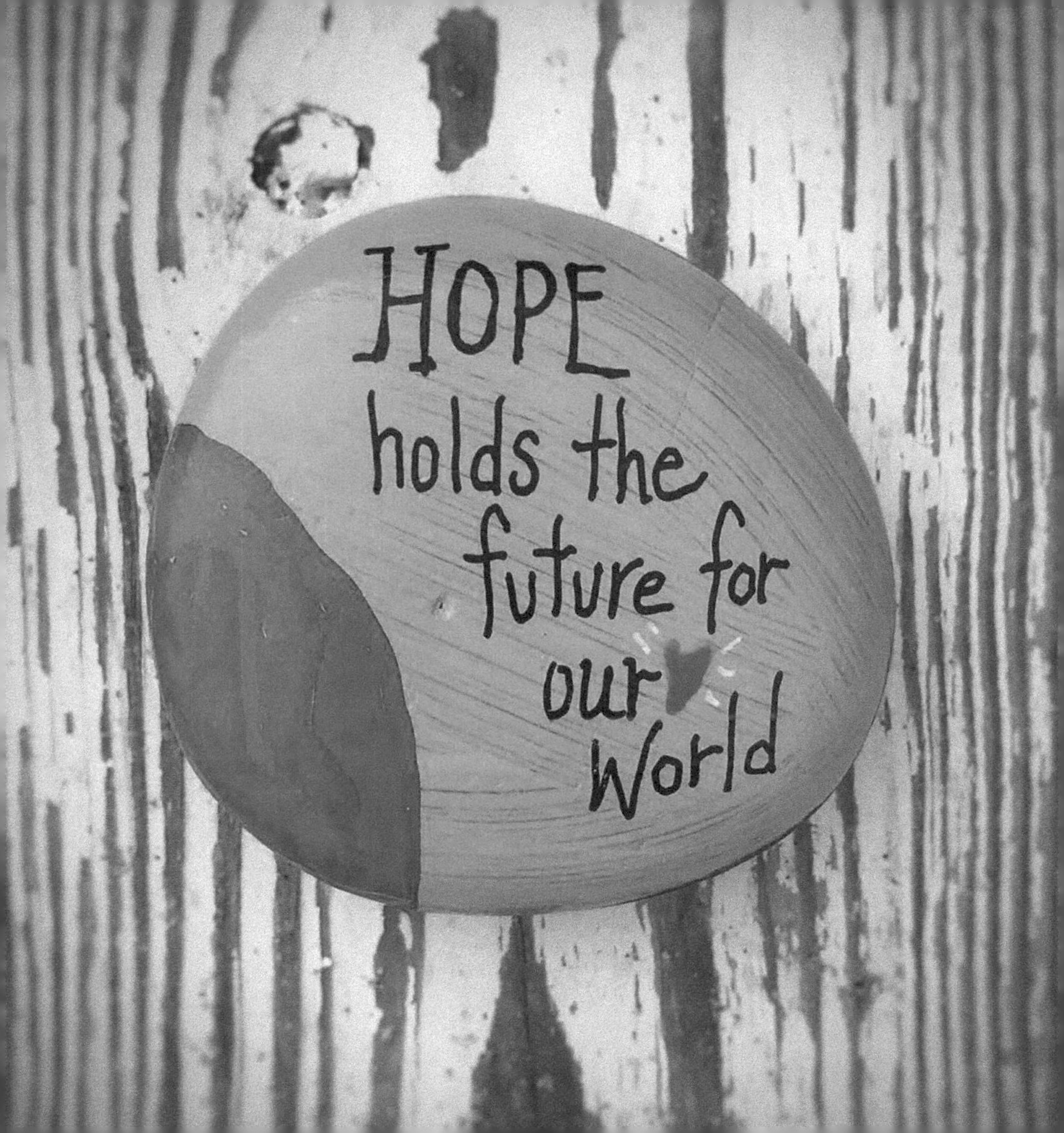
HOPE
holds the
future for
our
World

Hope Holds the Future for Our World

"Few things in the world are more powerful than a positive push. A smile. A world of optimism and hope. A 'you can do it' when things are tough."

—*Richard M. DeVos*

If It's Meant to Be, It Will Be

Sometimes, we must simply allow, after giving it our all, and praying, "let it be." There are moments—beyond our control—when there's a bigger plan for us! We just can't see it or understand the why. We must stay patient and trust that our why will unfold and come to us in due time.

The secret to getting ahead is simply by just getting Started!

The Secret to Getting Ahead Is Simply by Getting Started

"With each new day comes new strength and new thoughts."

—*Eleanor Roosevelt*

Lord, make me an instrument of thy peace. Where there is hatred let me sow love

Francis of Assisi

"Lord, Make Me An Instrument of Thy Peace. Where There Is Hatred Let Me Sow Love."

—Saint Francis of Assisi

Lord, make me an instrument of your peace,
where there is hatred let me sow love;
where there is injury, pardon;
where there is doubt, faith;
where there is despair, hope;
where there is sadness, joy.

Oh, divine master, grant that I may not so much seek
to be consoled as to console,
to be understood as to understand,
to be loved as to love.
For it is in giving that we receive
and it is in pardoning that we are pardoned
and it is in dying that we are born into eternal life.

—*Saint Francis of Assisi, "Peace Prayer"*

Nothing Is Inevitable

Nothing in life is inevitable. We may have a vision for what we hope our life will look like, however, situations arise and this vision may change along the way. By staying curious and remaining open to change, we remove any judgments and assumptions we may have. Embracing change can bring us great joy and help us evolve.

Live the way you want to be remembered

Live the Way You Want to Be Remembered

How would you like to be remembered? How many people would you like to touch in your short time here on Earth? If you knew you only had a few years left, how would you spend those days? What qualities would you like to be remembered for?

Chapter 5

Personal Growth

The way we treat others says alot about how we feel about ourselves.

The Way We Treat Others Says a Lot about How We Feel about Ourselves

There is so much truth in these words. When we are stressed out and life feels a bit overwhelming, we often become short with others. And when we are calm and content with things, we are kinder to those whom we come into contact with. The way we feel internally affects our relationships with others. It's no wonder that when we are anxious from the current events taking place in our world today, we then become anxious with each other. That is why kindness and compassion are needed now, and we must remain mindful of this fact!

"You Can Go Your Own Way."

—Fleetwood Mac

You can go "your own way" throughout life. Take the unconventional route. Put yourself out there, in the face of fear, or vulnerability or judgment. And as difficult as it will be sometimes, when you stay true to yourself and pay attention to your intuition amazing things happen. Things YOU were meant to do in this lifetime.

could it
Be that you play
a role in creating
your reality.

Could It Be That You Play a Role in Creating Your Reality?

This rock was created with the intention of giving a pause...or a thought moment for the recipient. So often, we remain steadfast in the notion that we are right, without considering the stance of another, and by doing so we lose that connection or we talk too much and don't take the time to simply listen to another. Maybe you are a giver, or a people pleaser at the expense of your own happiness? Whatever message you are meant to receive and reflect on is simply perfect...and meant just for you.

Breathe

"I wake up every day and I think, 'I'm breathing!' It's a good day."

—Eve Ensler

I Decide My Vibe

Repeat after me: I decide my vibe. In any given moment or situation, we get to decide our vibe! Do we wish to react from those free flying emotions that arise or respond thoughtfully and mindfully? The latter allows us to choose a response that has far greater benefits for our long term well-being.

Happiness
is
a state of mind

Happiness Is a State of Mind

"Happiness radiates like the fragrance from a flower and draws all good things toward you."

—*Maharishi Mahesh Yogi*

Balance

Balance is essential in order for us to feel fulfilled. Balance brings a sense
of order into our lives in work, life, and play; through our family, friends,
ourselves; within our mind, body, soul. When we look at these areas of our life,
we must recognize those areas where we are giving too much of our attention
to as well as the areas that we are neglecting. Often we are not conscious that
we are off balance until we are way out of whack and then we are forced to pay
attention. Make it a practice to check in on yourself now and again. Look at the
areas that are taking too much of your time, energy and attention and begin to
create a shift and find your equilibrium.

The things
that excite you
are not random.
They are connected to
your purpose.

Follow them.

The Things That Excite You Are Not Random. They Are Connected to Your Purpose. Follow Them.

Finding your purpose can seem overwhelming. What is your purpose anyway, you may ask?

Well, your purpose is that burning desire you have. It is that big reason that you are here on this planet at this time. All of us have our own unique purpose to fulfill. Some may find it early on while others may never uncover it in their lifetime. For those who do, you uncover a deeper purpose or meaning behind everything you do and life simply makes more sense in regards to your place in it. So how do you uncover this purpose of yours? Pay attention to the things that bring you joy and make you happy. They are clues that you are on the right path! And those things that seem off or just don't resonate with you are also clues that you may be off course. Next, get curious about everything—people, places, and things—like a child would. Learn, grow, expand and stretch yourself. Challenge all that you have learned or were taught. Are they expectations you are holding onto or fear of judgment from others that stops you from seeking it? It could be that ego of yours has fooled you into thinking you should remain where you are in the safety zone. Let it all go and you will find your purpose in no time.

Look for the beauty in everything and in everyone

Look for the Beauty in Everything and Everyone!

Often we find ourselves rushing from one thing to the next so often that we don't allow ourselves a moment to take in all of the beauty that surrounds us. We become immune to the simple pleasures such as long deep breathes of fresh air while walking on the beach or stopping to enjoy a moment of solitude while walking our dog. Maybe it's that person you meet by chance during your travels who says something that sparks an idea or a fond memory you have long forgotten about. We find ourselves exclaiming, like the character in *Alice in Wonderland*, "I'm late I'm late for a very important date!" The important moments often aren't found in the "dates," but in the little moments and spaces in between. The rides on the bus; the interaction with someone in line at the grocery store; your child as they share insight about their day. It's these little moments that we often don't give much attention to where beautiful inspiration and insights can be found. We view them as "on our way" moments or "when I get there" always thinking about the bigger event we are rushing toward. Today, maybe open yourself up to paying more attention to the spaces, the in-between moments and see the beauty that awaits.

Maybe Your Mess Is Really a Message!

Those darn growth moments. Why is it that they often arrive wrapped in one of life's messy moments or sticky situations? Well, that's because often we are given hints along the way to "turn back," to just say "no," or to "speak up." They come to us through our feelings based on our instincts, yet we often don't trust ourselves. We have self-doubt and we second guess these "signs." We disregard them and act or we don't take action accordingly. This similar situation will then present itself in our lives over and over again, until we pay attention to those same feelings that arise within us as a warning that something is "off." These situations may each look different as they come forward, but if we were to dissect them, we would find they hold the same message/lesson for our evolution. So these messes are actually blessings in some ways as they are simply leading us down a path that's meant for us. Approach the messy moments with an open mind and heart and grow with them!

Chapter 6

Self-Love

Creativity Takes Courage

Creativity takes courage. The courage to look at things through a unique perspective, YOUR unique perspective. It's all about adding your personal fingerprint to life. How amazing is it that we get to "create" our beautiful life? We each have something to accomplish in this lifetime...our paths are all very different and we must not fall into the trap of doing what everyone else is doing, because that may leave us feeling "lost" or without purpose. Get quiet, and allow your creativity to bubble up from within and explore all of life's amazing possibilities meant just for YOU.

There is magic in you, so abracadabra!

There Is Magic in You, So Abracadabra!

We all have a little bit of magic in us! Some of us uncover this magic and embrace it early in life while others continue to search for it. It may seem difficult to find because we do not know what we are looking for. It can be daunting. The secret to uncovering this magic is by paying attention to the things that bring you joy. It is in these people, places and experiences that you may pick up clues along the way. Next, become curious as to what about them makes you happy. Is it that you find inspiration and you lose track of time? Pay attention, take mental notes and begin to move in that direction. And finally, trust the process and remain patient. Soon, like a bolt of lightning, it will hit you!

Love

"Let us always meet each other with a smile, for the smile is the beginning of love."

—*Mother Teresa*

and
she just
knew that
EVERYTHING
would work
out

And She Just Knew That Everything Would Work Out

Because she had walked through many of life's storms and came out on the other side of them, she had all of the proof that she needed to know that everything would work out in the end.

When the Student is ready The teacher Will Appear.

Buddha

"When the Student Is Ready, the Teacher Will Appear."

—Buddha

Get quiet and embrace the teacher within.

self love
is my
Super power

Self-Love Is My Superpower

Self-love, believe it or not, IS a superpower! It all starts there. Without it, you may not possess the confidence, courage, conviction or motivation to follow whatever dream you have for YOUR life. In order to cultivate this self-love, start with simple awareness. Pay attention to those thoughts in that head of yours. Are they gentle and kind, destructive, or a little bit of both? Next become more mindful and if those thoughts are negative, simply change that thought pattern by paying attention to your breath. You cannot focus your attention on your breath and have thoughts at the same time. This will stop that negative thought in its tracks. Next, begin to speak to yourself with encouragement as you would in support of a friend. Finally write down all of your amazing qualities in a journal and each day return to reflect on them. Self-love is SO important. It truly is YOUR superpower!

because
she competes with
no one ~ no one can
compete with
her

"Because She Competes with No One, No One Can Compete with Her."

—Lao Tzu

We are taught as young children to "compete" with one another, to "be the best" or come in "first," but little emphasis was placed on our happiness. Competition can be good, of course, but only as a motivator for those things you love to do. There is not enough emphasis placed on finding those things that we enjoy. As children, we are placed in an educational/social environment that pushes each child along the same path. Being different than others makes us feel vulnerable and we are often viewed as weird. Imagine that? For many of us, it has taken too many years to get back to that place where we get to decide for ourselves what truly brings us joy! Some are still trying to figure this out, which is understandable! We have "played the game" and now it may be that time to figure it out for ourselves if we are going to compete with intention and purpose at something that we love!

Self-Love

On self-love…what a tumultuous relationship it is! One moment we are feeling proud and pleased with ourselves and, just like that, those feeling can turn on a dime. Out of nowhere we begin to feel insecure and question ourselves. Does this sound familiar? It truly is an interesting process and it happens to all of us…you are not alone. Curiosity is an important step in the process of self-love. We must first recognize our thoughts and the feelings they conjure up before we can begin to work through them. Most often, our self-doubt and fear arises from past experiences and we judge ourselves. We become self-critical. Now just imagine if we spoke to our friends and family the way we talk to ourselves. Would they feel supported and loved? Begin to make a shift by paying attention to your "self-talk" and replace any negativity with positive affirmations such as "I am brave," " I matter," "I am talented." These thoughts will fill your subconscious with positive emotions and, as time goes on, they will begin to replace and eliminate any negativity from popping up.

The greatness of a Man is not how much Wealth he acquires, but in his integrity & his ability to affect those around him positively.

"The Greatness of a Man Is Not How Much Wealth He Acquires But in His Integrity and His Ability to Affect Those around Him Positively."

—Bob Marley

How does one wish to be remembered? This is a question we must ask ourselves over and over again, especially when faced with a crossroads in our lives or when we are feeling unjustly criticized. When we approach these decisions or situations with integrity, understanding and kindness, we feel inner peace and reconciliation. When we are at peace, we are then able to spread that peace to those around us…and that is how we will then be remembered.

patience
my
dear
patience.

Patience, My Dear, Patience

"Patience, persistence and perspiration make an unbeatable combination for success."

—*Napoleon Hill*

Accentuate the Positive

By way of the law of attraction, when we look for positive things in our day, positive things will present themselves to us!

How to Join the Movement

"One moment can change a day, one day can change a life and one life can change the world!"

—*Buddha*

I hope you have enjoyed the inspiration found within these pages. Here at The Kindness Rocks Project, we believe that the perfect rock always seems to find the perfect person at just the right moment. It is truly amazing how one simple act of kindness, even represented through a small painted pebble, can make a huge impact on the life of another.

We also hope that you are now compelled to head out into your community and initiate kind acts in your own expressive way. If this book has inspired you in any way, we now call upon you to spread kindness in your community by painting it forward, because "one message at just the right moment can change someone's entire day, outlook, or life!" We hope you will join us.

Supplies Needed

- Smooth rocks

- Paper Towels

- Acrylic Paint (any bright color will do)

- Foam Paint Brush

- Oil-based Paint Pens

- Clear Sealant for top coat

ʳProduct suggestions can be found at www.thekindnessrocksproject.com

How To

Visit your local garden supply center for smooth river rocks. Rocks of 3"–5" work best. No need to worry about the color of the rock as you will be painting the surface with a cheery base coat.

Rinse the rocks in the sink to remove any dirt or salt and pat dry or allow them to dry on a paper towel.

Use a foam brush and your acrylic paint to paint one side of the rock creating a cheery canvas for your rock artwork. Allow to dry (you may need multiple coats depending on the color of the rock and the paint you are using).

While you are waiting for your rocks to dry, come up with your rock design or inspiration by thinking about messages that are uplifting and positive. Think about how finding your rock with this particular message could help someone who was feeling down.

Next, begin to write your message on the rock using your oil based paint pens.

Be sure to add on the back of your rock #thekindnessrocksproject so that when people find your rock they will post it online and you will be able to search the # to see if someone has found it and this will help you also connect with many kind likeminded people who have joined the project.

Once the paint pen artwork has dried completely, you can either paint on a top clear coat or lightly spray in a well ventilated area.

Allow this to dry for a few hours and, once dry, you are ready to spread some kindness with others. (Be sure to visit LNT.org for rules and regulations regarding Leave No Trace Principles.)

Follow us on Facebook, Instagram and Twitter and sign up for our email list at www.thekindnessrocksproject.com for updates on the project and to receive a weekly Inspirational Rock Message created just for you!

Acknowledgments

This book is dedicated to all of the kind souls who have joined The Kindness Rocks Project. Thank you for opening your courageous hearts and joining our grassroots kindness movement. Without all of your love and support this project would simply be the hobby of one. Also for my Mom and Dad, Raymond and Phyllis Moloney, who continue to support and guide me from above leaving divine signs and messages along the beaches of Cape Cod.

To my core team of talented supporters Jason, Carol, Roberta, Marc, Manx, Janet, Pam, Chris, and Sarah who believed in me and supported the project from its inception by offering their unique talents. And last but not least, for my supportive husband Matt and my three wonderful daughters, Molly, Maggie and Madelyn, who inspire me each and every day to strive to be a better mother, wife, friend and all around human being.

Megan Murphy

Megan Murphy is the founder of The Kindness Rocks Project, a grassroots kindness movement that has swept the nation and beyond. She is a women's empowerment coach, business mentor with S.C.O.R.E., Kindness Activist, freelance writer, meditation instructor and inspirational speaker. She resides on Cape Cod, MA with her husband, three daughters, and two giant dogs.

Megan is a Certified Professional Coach (CPC) and a certified business mentor earning her coaching certifications through the Institute for Professional Excellence in Coaching (IPEC) and is a member of the International Coaching Federation ICF.

The Kindness Rocks Project has been featured on Fox News Boston, NBC Boston, WCVB Channel 5's "5 for Good" segment, *The Boston Globe*, *The Detroit Free Press*, *The Washington Post*, *Cape Cod Life* magazine, *Conscious Lifestyle Magazine*, *Parents* magazine, the *Cape Cod Times*, Today.com, *The Huffington Post*, *Southern Living* magazine, *Country Living* magazine, and many other regional news media outlets across the country where members of the project participate. Megan has been published in the 2017 *Chicken Soup for the Soul: My Kind (of) America* book; *MindBodyGreen*; Tut.com, Grown & Flown, and quoted in many more publications, podcasts, and blogs. For more information about The Kindness Rocks Project visit www.TheKindnessRocksProject.com and Megan Murphy visit www.MeganMurphyCoaching.com.

Printed in the USA
CPSIA information can be obtained
at www.ICGtesting.com
JSHW072028140824
68134JS00044B/3830

9 781633 539501